D0579602

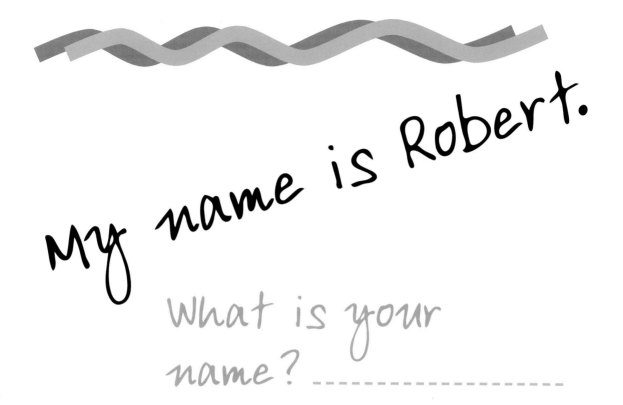

My name is Robert.

What is your name? _____

Grandpa has changed

Pam Pollack & Meg Belviso
Illustrations: Marta Fàbrega

BARRON'S

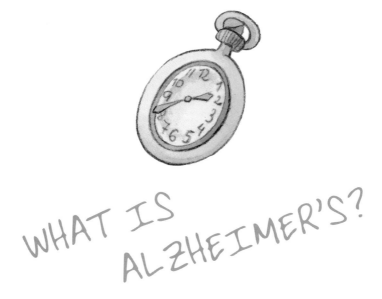

WHAT IS ALZHEIMER'S?

Today is Saturday and, just like every week, we're going to visit Grandpa at his house.

A few days ago, Mom told us that Grandpa is suffering from an illness called Alzheimer's. Although he wants to keep living in his house, he might decide to come live with us later.

That's why we're going to learn about the illness, in order to help him.

IT'S A MATTER OF MEMORY

"Mom, Grandpa doesn't look sick," I said to her.
"People with Alzheimer's don't look sick, but the illness makes them forget things," Mom replied.
"Can kids catch Alzheimer's too, like they catch a cold?" asked Jane, my little sister.
"No," Mom replied. "Only elderly people can get Alzheimer's."

THE STORY OF THE ICE CREAM

Grandpa is my best friend.
Since he has the illness, he sometimes
does funny things. Once he forgot
how to get to the grocery store.
Sometimes he forgets my name,
even though I'm named after him.
Then there was the time when we
got ice cream at the store. Grandpa
put the ice cream in the mailbox,
and put the mail in the freezer.

WE WANT TO KEEP PLAYING WITH GRANDPA...

Mom said that Grandpa went to the doctor because he kept forgetting things. After doing some tests on him, the doctor explained that his brain wasn't working as it should.

This Saturday, Jane and I were very anxious. If he's sick, will he be in bed all the time?

Will he be able to play with us?

On the way to his house, we remembered the first day that
Grandpa took us fishing and taught us his special trick:
"If you whistle," he told us, "they always bite."
I didn't believe it at first, but we whistled and it worked.
Even my little sister caught one! And when we went back home,
Grandpa made us a whole meal with the fish: It was delicious!

GRANDPA'S SPECIAL TRICK

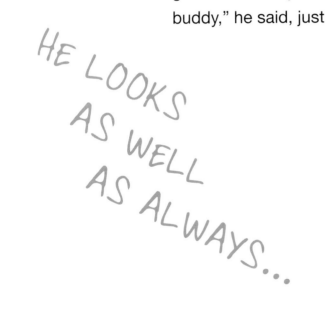

When we got to Grandpa's house a nice lady opened the door. It was Grandpa's nurse. "Nice to meet you," she said. "My name is Helen." We all said, "Hello, Helen." Grandpa was wearing his pajamas and bathrobe, and he looked the same as always. However, he also had a pair of fancy shiny boots on. I guess that was OK. He gave me and my little sister a big hug. "Hey buddy," he said, just like he always did.

HE LOOKS AS WELL AS ALWAYS...

GRANDPA STILL CAN PLAY CATCH!

Mom gave Grandpa some flowers from our garden.
Jane showed him a picture she drew. I gave him
some photos of me playing ball with my team.
"Maybe we can play catch in the yard later,"
said Grandpa. "I bet you've gotten pretty good."

WE CAN DO SOME THINGS TO HELP HIS MEMORY

After lunch Grandpa and I played catch.
Then we sat on the porch, and Jane
and I told Grandpa about school. Helen
came out with some photo albums that
we had brought with us.
"Why don't you look through these?"
she said. "Looking at pictures can help
your grandfather's memory."
We all looked at photo albums. There were
lots of pictures of me and my sister with
Grandpa at his house.
"What a pretty picture," said Grandpa.
"When was that taken?"
"That picture is from my birthday," my little
sister said very seriously.
Grandpa looked confused.

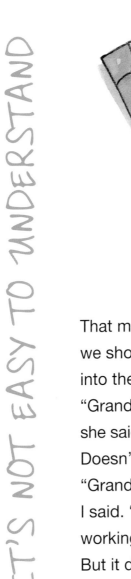

IT'S NOT EASY TO UNDERSTAND

That made Jane upset. Mom said
we should take a walk. I took her out
into the yard.
"Grandpa doesn't remember anything,"
she said. "How could he forget my birthday?
Doesn't he love me anymore?"
"Grandpa loves us just like he always did,"
I said. "He's just sick. His brain isn't
working right. It can't remember things.
But it doesn't mean he doesn't love us."
"I love him too," said my sister.

WE'LL MAYBE GO FISHING AGAIN!

We went back to the house. Grandpa was still looking
at the photo album. He pointed to a picture. "This is from
the time we went fishing!" he said.

"That's right, Grandpa," I said. It looked like the photo
albums were a good idea! "You taught us to whistle
to catch the fish."

"I'd sure like to go fishing again," said Grandpa.
"Maybe we'll go next weekend."

When it was time to leave, neither my little sister nor
I wanted to go. We gave Grandpa a big hug. Mom gave
Helen a hug too. "Thank you for helping my father,"
she said.

GRANDPA NEEDS OUR HELP

On the way home we stopped
for ice cream.
"I wish things were the way they
used to be," Jane said. "I wish
Grandpa was still the same.
I wish he wasn't sick."
"I wish Grandpa wasn't sick too,"
Mom said. "But we can
remember the fun we had
together. And we can also help
him in many ways."

ON OUR WAY TO THE LAKE

Next week we arrived at Grandpa's home very early. Grandpa was smiling and wearing his fishing outfit. He also had a big red tie and boots that didn't match, which was a bit strange, but we just smiled.

Mom leaned down to whisper to us. "Don't worry. If Grandpa gets confused, we'll help him."

And so we went to the lake.

TRYING
TO REMEMBER

When we arrived, Grandpa looked at the water, the tall trees, the big clouds, and he just stood there.

Mom came close to him. "Is everything OK?" she asked.

Grandpa was sad. "I am not sure if I've been here before," he said. "Have I?"

"Not right here. I think we used to go behind those trees," said Mom.

"Yes, that must be it," whispered Grandpa.

WE ARE A GREAT TEAM!

We sat on the dock and started
fishing. But we got no bites for
a long time.
Then I saw Grandpa smile.
He looked at me, and said,
"Perhaps they'll come if we whistle."
Mom was happy. "Dad! You
remembered!" Then she turned
away and I saw she had tears.
So we whistled. We whistled a lot.
And the fish started to bite!

Activities

PLAY THE BRAIN GAME

Have you ever wondered how the brain tells your body what to do? In the brain there are thousands of tiny hairy blobs called neurons (NYOOR-ons). Neurons pass the information from one to the other. What kind of information? Imagine if you put your hand on a hot stove. Your fingers would send a message to the neurons in your brain. The message would be: HOT! The neurons would tell you to pull your hand away from the stove. It would happen so fast you wouldn't even know it.

Let's play a game that shows us how neurons work. Stand in a circle with your friends or family. Each person in the circle is like a neuron. One person writes a message on a piece of paper. Let's say the message is: CLUCK LIKE A CHICKEN. Fold up the piece of paper and pass it from your left hand to the right hand of the person beside you. That person passes the paper from one hand to the other, and then to the next person.

The message goes all around the circle until the person who wrote the message yells, "Stop!" Whoever is holding the piece of paper reads the message. Then they must do whatever the message says. It's time to cluck like a chicken!

The person who got the message gets to write a message for someone else. How about pretending to be a dog and begging for food?

Now imagine if someone left the circle. How would the message get passed along? It wouldn't. That is what happens when someone has Alzheimer's. The neurons can't pass messages to and from the brain.

Even though people with Alzheimer's can't do everything they did before, there are a lot of things you can enjoy with them. In fact, doing things with other people helps people with Alzheimer's because it puts their brain into action.

Here are ten ways to have fun with a person with Alzheimer's:
1. Read your favorite books out loud to each other.
2. See who can finish the most famous sayings like "The early bird catches the…"
3. If you have a pet, play with it together.
4. Sing old songs and dance together.
5. Look at family pictures and tell what you recall about them.
6. Play hangman.
7. Talk about your favorite fictional characters.
8. Play electronic puzzle games.
9. Write a poem together.
10. Give them a hug.

THE MEMORY BOOK

People with Alzheimer's often can talk—but don't—because they forget things. A memory book can help these people remember simple facts about themselves, like where they were born and who is in their family. This makes them feel more confident about talking to other people. Memory books also help their friends and relatives, because they don't have to ask the same question over and over.

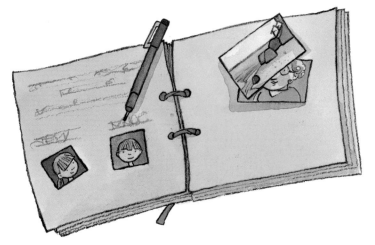

HOW TO MAKE A MEMORY BOOK

1. With the help of an adult, punch two holes in pages of construction paper.

2. Run a ribbon through the holes to attach the papers together.

3. On each page of construction paper paste an index card with a fact on it. For instance, "What are the names of my grandchildren?" Under the question, write the answer. If you can, use a picture to help them remember. For instance, under your name, put a picture of yourself.

Find a picture of the hometown of the person with Alzheimer's. Paste it. On top of the page, write "Where was I born?" Then write about the town and its people beneath the picture

On another page write important dates for the week and month: "When are my grandchildren coming to visit?" "My grandchildren come to visit me every Saturday afternoon." Then continue with other useful information.

4. If the person with Alzheimer's is in a wheelchair, have an adult help you cut a strip of Velcro and attach it to the book. Attach another strip to the arm of the wheelchair.

Parent's guide

The purpose of this book is to acknowledge the presence of people with Alzheimer's in the lives of children and to recognize some of the realities of this disease that children may face. The following information was obtained from the U.S. National Library of Medicine, the National Institute of Health, and the Alzheimer's Association.

What is Alzheimer's?
Alzheimer's is the most common form of dementia in people over 65. Cells in the parts of the brain responsible for learning, reasoning, and memory become clogged with tangled masses of protein fibers. Alzheimer's is the fourth leading cause of death after heart disease, cancer, and stroke.

Signs and symptoms: early stages
The ten most common warning signs of Alzheimer's are:
   1. Memory loss. A person forgets things more often and can't recall the information later.
   2. Difficulty in performing familiar tasks. People find it hard to perform tasks that require thought, even if they used to do them easily. For instance, they may lose track of the steps to make a meal or forget how to balance a checkbook.
   3. Language problems. Familiar words are forgotten or replaced. For instance, they might call a hairbrush "that thing for my head."
   4. Disorientation. People with Alzheimer's can become lost even in a familiar area, forgetting how they got there or how to get home.
   5. Poor judgment. A person might dress inappropriately for the weather.
   6. Problems with abstract thinking. People have trouble with complex mental tasks, like forgetting how to use numbers to solve a problem.
   7. Misplacing things. They may put things in unusual places, like ice cream in the mailbox.
   8. Mood and behavior changes. Mood swings come and go for no reason.
   9. Changes in personality. The personality can change dramatically.
10. Loss of initiative. A person may lose interest in activities he or she previously enjoyed.

Signs and symptoms: more advanced stages

At the later stages patients have difficulty in picking out clothing and getting dressed. They may lose awareness of who they are and be unable to make meals or drive a car. In late stages of Alzheimer's, language is impaired and patients have trouble recognizing family members.

Lifestyle changes

There is no cure for Alzheimer's. The goals of treatment are to make the patient comfortable, minimize confusion, and slow the disease's progression. Some things that Alzheimer's patients can do to help themselves include taking regular walks with a caregiver and listening to calming music. Having a pet dog is also helpful, as long as there is someone else to look after the animal. It is very important to include the patients in their own treatment. Try to understand how they perceive their world and give them a chance to talk about what they are dealing with.

Children and Alzheimer's

Dealing with a loved one who has Alzheimer's can be confusing and scary for children. It is important to address their fears before they make their own assumptions about what is going on.

If a child is very young, it's not necessary to use the term *Alzheimer's disease*. Explain that the loved one is sick, has trouble remembering things, and might sometimes be confused. It's important to explain that the person will get sicker and that he or she will need the family's help. If you can, prepare them for the changes they will see in the loved one.

Children are liable to have strong feelings about the situation. Make sure they know these feelings are acceptable. Assure them that their loved one still loves them and appreciates their company. Tell them to accept the fact that the person they love will feel angry or sad or miss the way things used to be. If visits become too painful for children, don't force them to continue.

Some emotions that children might have are:
- Fear that their parents or even they might get Alzheimer's.
- Anxiety, sadness, or fear in response to the loved one's change in personality.
- Frustration over having to repeat themselves or remind the loved one of basic facts.
- Remorse over being impatient or frustrated with their loved one.
- Self-consciousness about being out in public with a sick person.
- Shame about having an Alzheimer's patient living at home with them.

If a child is experiencing any of these feelings, he or she will not necessarily talk about them. Sometimes children will act out, get distracted from schoolwork, avoid the family... If this happens, try to talk to them about their feelings and behavior.

We hope this book will help families and children to adapt to a loved one with Alzheimer's.

GRANDPA HAS CHANGED

First edition for the United States and Canada
published in 2009 by
Barron's Educational Series, Inc.

© Copyright 2009 by Gemser Publications S.L.
El Castell, 38; Teià (08329) Barcelona, Spain
(World Rights)

Title of the original in Spanish:
El abuelito ha cambiado

Author: Pam Pollack and Meg Belviso

Illustrator: Marta Fàbrega

All inquiries should be addressed to:
Barron's Educational Series, Inc.
250 Wireless Boulevard
Hauppauge, NY 11788
www.barronseduc.com

ISBN-13: 978-0-7641-4282-6
ISBN-10: 0-7641-4282-8

Library of Congress
Control Number 2008938301

Printed in China

9 8 7 6 5 4 3 2 1